The Fact-Packed ACTIVITY Book
SHARKS
AND OTHER SEA CREATURES

Editors Srijani Ganguly, Abi Maxwell
US Senior Editor Shannon Beatty
Senior Art Editor Kanika Kalra
Project Art Editor Charlotte Jennings
Assistant Art Editor Nishtha Gupta
DTP Designers Syed Md Farhan, Dheeraj Singh
Picture Research Administrator Vagisha Pushp
Senior Jacket Art Editor Dheeraj Arora
Production Editor Dragana Puvacic
Production Controller Rebecca Parton
Deputy Managing Editor Roohi Sehgal
Managing Editors Monica Saigal, Jonathan Melmoth
Managing Art Editors Ivy Sengupta,
Diane Peyton Jones
Delhi Creative Head Malavika Talukder
Art Director Mabel Chan
Managing Director Sarah Larter

Consultant Dr. Kim Dennis-Bryan

Material in this publication was previously published in:
*Ultimate Factivity Collection: Sharks, Dolphins,
and other Sea Creatures* (2015)

First American Edition, 2024
Published in the United States by DK Publishing,
a division of Penguin Random House LLC
1745 Broadway, 20th Floor, New York, NY 10019

A catalog record for this book
is available from the Library of Congress.
ISBN 978-0-7440-9906-5

DK books are available at special discounts when purchased
in bulk for sales promotions, premiums, fund-raising,
or educational use. For details, contact: DK Publishing Special
Markets, 1745 Broadway, 20th Floor, New York, NY 10019
SpecialSales@dk.com

Printed and bound in China

www.dk.com

MIX
Paper | Supporting
responsible forestry
FSC™ C018179

This book was made with Forest
Stewardship Council™ certified
paper—one small step in DK's
commitment to a sustainable future.
Learn more at
www.dk.com/uk/information/sustainability

Contents

How this book works

Here is some information to help you find your way around this book, which is all about sharks and other sea creatures.

Activities
There are many exciting activities for you to do in this book. All you need is a pen or pencil, crayons, a little imagination, and a thirst for knowledge!

These boxes give fun facts about topics.

Look for this roundel on every spread. It tells you what the activity is.

MATCH
the mythical creatures to their pictures. Check your answers on pp. 92–93.

Answers
The answers to the questions are on pp. 92–93. Good luck!

Instructions
All the instructions you'll need to complete an activity can be found on each page.

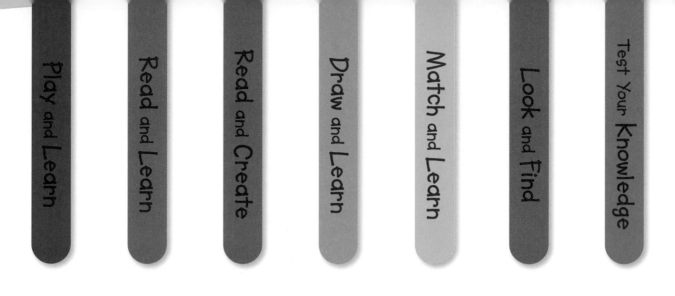

These are the different types of activity that you will find in the book:

1 **Play and Learn:** Follow the lines or join the dots to discover more about different marine animals.

2 **Read and Learn:** Read the information on the pages to learn more.

3 **Read and Create:** After reading the pages, use your coloring pens or pencils to color the pictures.

4 **Draw and Learn:** Get ready with your pencils to draw, learn, and have fun.

5 **Match and Learn:** Match the descriptions to the pictures.

6 **Look and Find:** Let's see how well you can spot the pictures in the book.

7 **Test Your Knowledge:** Test yourself by answering mind-boggling questions, and see if you've guessed correctly.

Introductions give you an overview of the topic that is being discussed on the pages.

Amazing activities will help you understand a specific topic better.

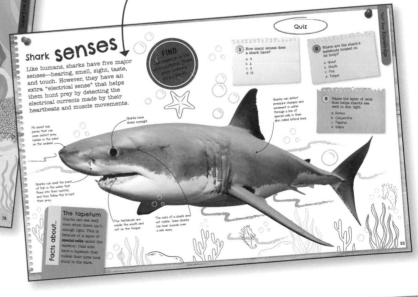

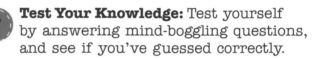

The world beneath the waves

We may live on the land, but most of our planet is covered in ocean: a huge, mysterious environment full of amazing and diverse wildlife. How much do you know about it?

FIND

where these pictures are on pp. 8–25. Check your answers on pp. 92–93.

7

8

9

10

11

12

What do you know about the Ocean?

There are so many fascinating things to learn about the ocean. Test your knowledge to see if you can identify the true facts from the false ones!

1 About 90 percent of the world's oxygen is produced in the ocean.

2 Moon jellyfish have translucent bells. This means you can see straight through them.

3 The famous, swordlike tusk belonging to the narwhal is actually an overgrown nose.

4 There are about 3 million shipwrecks on the ocean floor.

5 The deepest oceanic trench is the Mariana Trench. It's more than 6,562 ft (2,000 m) deeper than the entire height of Mount Everest!

GUESS
if these eight statements are true or false. Answers on pp. 92–93.

6 Orcas gather in large pods of more than 85 individuals.

7 The Ring of Fire is a path of more than 450 volcanoes along the Pacific Ocean.

8 The ocean's biggest fish is the whale shark, which can weigh as much as 40 tons (36 metric tons).

Facts about...

Undiscovered species
The ocean is so big that much of it is still a **mystery**. Scientists believe that the world's oceans are home to several million different species of animals and plants.

Polar bears are marine mammals. They spend much of their time in Arctic waters and on the sea ice.

Indian Ocean

The Indian Ocean is the **warmest** of the five oceans. It lies to the south of Asia, and separates Australia and Africa.

India

Africa

Australia

Arctic Ocean

North America

North Pole

Europe

The Arctic is the **smallest** of the five oceans, and is partly covered in sea ice for most of the year. At the North Pole, the surface waters of the Arctic ocean are frozen all year round.

The blue planet

The Earth is known as the "blue planet" because so much of it is covered by the oceans. These huge bodies of water are home to many of the strangest and most amazing creatures on Earth.

FIND the answers to the quiz questions. Check your answers on pp. 92–93.

Oceans cover more than 70 percent of the Earth's surface.

Facts about...

World ocean

Although there are five different oceans on Earth, they're all connected, forming a **global ocean** that contains more than 97 percent of all the water on Earth.

Atlantic Ocean

Separating Europe, the Americas, and Africa, the Atlantic is the **second largest** of the oceans and covers almost 20 percent of the Earth's surface.

Europe

North America

Africa

South America

Sharks can be found in all five oceans.

Penguins are excellent swimmers. Most of them are found in or near the Southern Ocean.

Southern Ocean

South Africa

South America

Antarctica

Australia

Surrounding the South Pole and Antarctica, the Southern Ocean is the only ocean that **stretches all around the globe**.

North America

Pacific Ocean

Covering more than 30 percent of the Earth's surface, the Pacific is by far the **biggest** ocean on the planet. With a maximum depth of around 36,070 ft (10,994 m), it's also the **deepest ocean on Earth**.

South America

Australia

QUIZ

1 Which continent is surrounded by the Southern Ocean?

2 Which ocean is the smallest of the five?

3 What is the maximum depth of the Pacific Ocean?

4 What percentage of the Earth's surface does the Atlantic Ocean cover?

5 Which ocean is the warmest of the five?

What lives in the ocean?

All life on Earth first began in the ocean, and today, millions of years later, the ocean is still home to more than half of all of Earth's known species.

Cnidarians
Pronounced "nyedarian" and best known for their stinging tentacles, these creatures have existed for millions of years.

Corals and sea anemones

Barnacles

Jellyfish

Shrimp, crabs, and lobsters

Sponges
These animals are very simple life forms. The adults usually stay rooted in one place or creep along very slowly.

Feather duster worms

Demospongia

Bearded fireworms

Hydroid

Sea spiders

Tubular

Christmas tree worms

Brine shrimp

Arthropods
This is the same group that insects belong to. There are more species of arthropod than any other animal on Earth.

TRUE OR FALSE?
SOME SPONGES CAN MOVE AROUND.

Worms
These simple creatures have soft bodies and no limbs. There are many different types.

Invertebrates

Separating species

While there are millions of species on Earth, they all fall into one of two categories—invertebrates (those without backbones) and vertebrates (those with backbones).

Facts about...

The larger group

Although almost every animal we would recognize is a vertebrate, there are actually **far more invertebrates** on Earth in total.

Sharks and rays

Echinoderms
The bodies of these creatures point outward from their center. They are only ever found in water.

Sea urchins

Chordates
Most animals we think of are chordates. This includes all land and marine mammals, birds, reptiles, and fish.

Brittle stars

Sea cucumbers

Sea stars

Whales and dolphins

Clams, oysters, and scallops

Feather stars

Mammals, such as seals

Reptiles, such as turtles

Octopuses, squid, and cuttlefish

READ
about the different kinds of creatures found in the oceans.

Bony fish

Sea slugs and snails

Mollusks
The second largest group of animals, mollusks have soft bodies, but some are covered in hard shells.

Vertebrates

Underwater habitats

A habitat is an environment in which an organism naturally lives. Just like there are a variety of habitats on land, there are different kinds of underwater habitats where marine life flourishes.

FIND

the answers to the quiz questions. Check your answers on pp. 92–93.

Open oceans

The largest habitat on Earth, the open ocean has different zones with varying levels of light, temperature, and pressure. Most marine life, such as whales, oceanic sharks, and plankton, live in the sunlit upper zones. The cold, dark depths are home to strange fish, octopuses, and crustaceans.

A humpback whale leaping out of the water

A group of walruses

Cold polar seas

The Arctic and Southern oceans near the Poles have icy waters. Although the water is frozen in places, these oceans teem with marine life. Some of the creatures found here include polar bears, walruses, and krill.

Facts about...

Polar fish

Most fish that live in the polar regions produce **antifreeze chemicals** in their blood. This prevents them from freezing in the cold waters.

A shanny in a rock pool

Tide pool

When the ocean retreats during a low tide, small pools of seawater called tide pools are left behind on rocky shores. Creatures such as shanny, limpets, and cape rock crabs live here. They can survive both in and out of water.

A colorful coral reef

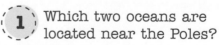

Coral reefs

Coral reefs are huge, colorful structures that look like underwater gardens. Although the reefs cover only a small part of the ocean, they are home to a wide range of fish and other marine creatures.

Quiz

1. Which two oceans are located near the Poles?

2. In which habitat do whales and oceanic sharks live?

3. What do coral reefs look like?

4. Where can tide pools be found?

Busy Coral reefs

Coral reefs are beautiful underwater worlds made from lots of tiny animals that join together to make large colonies. These colonies are brimming with life, and many different marine species call them their home.

Reef shark

Cuttlefish

Yellowtail snapper

Blue tang

Giant clam

Trumpet fish

Clown triggerfish

Beaked leatherjacket

Moray eel

Fan worm

Sea star

Facts about...

A giant reef
The Great Barrier Reef off the coast of Australia is the **largest coral reef in the world**. It's home to thousands of creatures, and is so big that it can be seen from space.

Eagle ray

Reefs are full of little cracks for marine life to hide in.

COLOR
all of the animals living among the coral reef. Look closely— some are hiding!

Sea turtle

Table coral

Parrotfish

Long finned coralfish

Pink sea fan

Rainforests of the sea

Coral reefs contain about 25 percent of all marine life on Earth, despite only covering about 0.1 percent of the ocean's seabed.

Staghorn coral

Seahorse

Beaked coralfish

Clown fish

Brain coral

Sea anemone

Facts about...

Coral
Though it looks like rock, coral is made up of thousands of tiny animals called **polyps**, some of which develop a hard skeleton to protect their soft bodies.

Daisy coral

Yum. Sea urchins are one of my favourite foods!

Underwater jungle

START

Kelp is a tough seaweed. It can grow very tall and create underwater jungles called kelp forests. These areas are often filled with many marine animals, including sea otters. They are also home to sea urchins, the pesky pests that eat the kelp.

Sea otters

These mammals dive down to catch and eat sea urchins. They may not know it, but by doing this they're helping to protect the entire forest and the animals it provides food and shelter to.

DRAW

a route through the kelp to help the otter reach the sea urchins.

Facts about...

Kelp

Underwater kelp forests can grow very quickly—up to 24 in (60 cm) a day. The largest forests can reach **massive heights** of 174 ft (53 m) under suitable conditions.

Sea urchins

These little creatures devour
the coastal kelp forests in
California, leaving the area
almost barren. If it wasn't for
sea otters, they might destroy
so much of the forest that it
would harm the creatures that
live there.

FINISH

19

Polar waters

At the top and bottom of the planet are the freezing Arctic and Southern oceans. You might think these icy cold waters are empty, but they are actually home to a lot of marine life.

FIND the answers to the quiz questions. Check your answers on pp. 92–93.

Slender **Arctic cod** are a rich source of food for many marine animals in colder waters.

Beluga whales are white in color and have a thick layer of blubber that keeps them warm.

Arctic Ocean

The tusks of a **Pacific walrus** can grow to up to 3 ft (1 m) long. Like the tusks of elephants, these are made of a hard substance called ivory.

Facts about...

Krill

These **tiny crustaceans** are possibly one of the most **abundant species** of animal on Earth. They are a very important food source for marine life.

Quiz

1 Penguins are mostly found on which continent?

a. Antarctica
b. Asia
c. North America
d. Europe

2 How long can the tusks of a Pacific walrus grow?

a. Up to 492 ft (150 m)
b. Up to 66 ft (20 m)
c. Up to 23 ft (7 m)
d. Up to 3 ft (1 m)

3 Which crustacean is one of the most abundant animals on Earth?

a. Krill
b. Crab
c. Shrimp
d. Lobster

4 What color are beluga whales?

a. Green
b. Pink
c. White
d. Purple

Penguins are birds that can't fly, but they're very good swimmers. Most are found on the continent of Antarctica in the cold Southern Ocean.

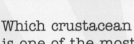

Southern Ocean

Leopard seals are fierce predators. These spotted seals eat octopuses, penguins, and even other seals!

Native to the Antarctic and subantarctic waters, **hourglass dolphins** usually swim in groups of up to 14.

Found near the North Pole, **polar bears** are very strong swimmers. They can hold their breath underwater for more than three minutes!

READ

about the different ocean zones and the creatures that live in them.

Sunlit zone: 0–656 ft (0–200 m)

Nearly all marine animals, such as the Pacific sea nettle jellyfish, live here. This is the part of the ocean where the sunlight is the brightest. Organisms that produce food using the sun's energy and animals that surface regularly to breathe are found here.

Lanternshark

My large eyes help me see in poor light.

Midnight zone: 3,280–13,123 ft (1,000–4,000 m)

Hydrothermal vents are found in this zone that release hot water rich in minerals. These minerals are processed by bacteria, which are then eaten by creatures such as shrimp, crabs, and clams that live here. This zone is in total darkness, so creatures such as the dumbo octopus hunt for prey that glow in the dark.

Sea pen

I may look like a plant, but I'm actually an animal.

Ocean Zones

From the surface to the seafloor, the ocean can be divided into zones based on depth. Each zone is darker and emptier than the one above. Since the upper layers receive more sunlight and are warmer, most life is found there.

TRUE OR FALSE?
THE HADAL ZONE IS THE MOST WELL-LIT AREA OF THE OCEAN.

Sunfish

My tentacles are venomous.

Pacific sea nettle jellyfish

Twilight zone: 656–3,280 ft (200–1,000 m)

Most fish live in this zone. Many of the animals that live here are able to create their own faint light source. For example, lanternsharks have specific cells that are able to glow in the dark.

Dumbo octopus

I have big, earlike fins.

Facts about...

Black smokers

Sometimes minerals rise up through the ocean floor and harden into **chimneylike shapes**. These unusual structures are known as black smokers.

Abyssal zone: 13,123–19,685 ft (4,000–6,000 m)

There is hardly any food for the animals that survive in this extremely cold, dark zone. While sea pens and tripodfish wait for food to float to them, bone-eating worms and giant isopods feed on dead animals.

I'm a close relative of shrimp.

Deep-sea amphipod

Hadal zone: 19,685–36,090 ft (6,000–11,000 m)

The ocean floor is a desolate darkness. The few creatures that live here, such as the deep-sea amphipod, survive in the extreme conditions by feasting on the bodies of dead animals that sink down from above.

Stars of the sea

Sea stars are sometimes called starfish, but they are not fish. They are "echinoderms"—like sea cucumbers or sea urchins. Sea stars have the useful ability to regrow lost limbs, and sometimes even their entire bodies.

Horned sea star
Its body is covered in rows of large spikes or "horns" that keep predators away.

Common sea star
This sea star is often orange but can also be purple or brown.

Common sunstar
The common sun star has short arms, but can have a large number of them.

Necklace sea star
This sea star varies in color a lot, but it always lives in shallow water.

Sea stars can be many different colors, including blue, red, and orange.

DRAW and color your own sea star in the space above.

Marine **creatures**

The ocean is full of fascinating animals. From colorful and striking fish to smart and social dolphins, all kinds of creatures live here.

1

2

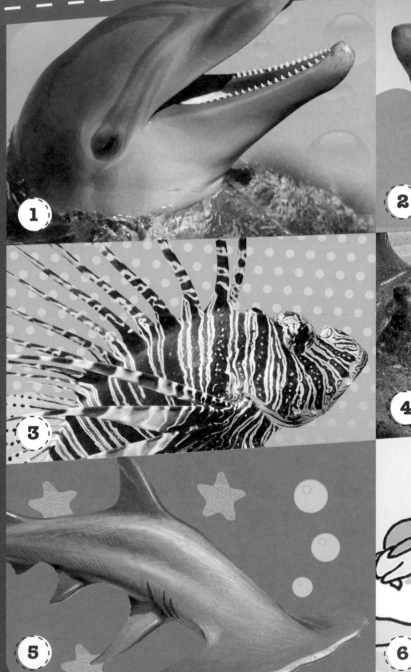

3

4

5

6

FIND

where these pictures are on pp. 28–45. Check your answers on pp. 92–93.

7

8

9

10

11

12

What's my job?

The world's oceans are so big that there's so much we still don't know about them. But many people dedicate their lives to studying the oceans and the creatures that live there.

MATCH each job to the description. Check your answers on pp. 92–93.

1 I take **pictures of the marine environment and the creatures** that live there using my special camera.

a Marine archeologist

d Marine biologist

2 I study the different physical features of the ocean along with the **marine animals** that live in it.

b Fisherman

3 I use a variety of **underwater equipment**. Some are vessels that accommodate humans, and others are robotic.

28

4 I help to **protect the ocean and its wildlife** from harm, and clean up pollution.

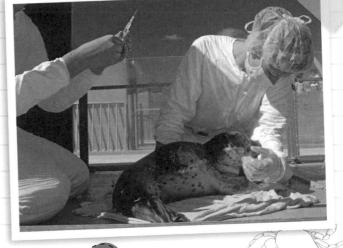

f Marine vet

c Marine photographer

5 I investigate **shipwrecks and study ancient objects** that are submerged in water.

6 I sail the oceans **catching fish** for people to eat.

g Deep-sea ecologist

7 I **take care of sick animals** that live in the oceans, zoos, and aquariums.

e Marine conservationist

29

What is a fish?

The world's oceans have been filled with fish for more than 500 million years. Today, we know of about 36,000 different species.

A fishy checklist

Because fish live underwater, they move and breathe differently than land animals. But almost all fish—no matter how different they seem—have five things in common.

Fish bodies are often protected by plates made of thin, bone–like substances called scales.

Instead of lungs, fish breathe underwater through organs called gills.

Sailfin snapper

Fins are primarily used for swimming. The tail fin propels the fish forward. The other fins are used for steering and orientation.

The majority of fish are cold-blooded, and their bodies stay the same temperature as the water around them.

Most fish have a skeleton made of bone, but sharks and rays have skeletons made of cartilage.

Diversity

Fish come in an extraordinary range of shapes, colors, and sizes. The biggest fish, the whale shark, can grow to be 62 ft (19 m) long, and one of the smallest fish, the dwarf pygmy goby, is just ⅜ in (1 cm) long!

Queen triggerfish

Fire goby

Clown fish

Angelfish

Cuckoo wrasse

Porcupine fish

Foxface rabbitfish

Lionfish

Pollack

Polka dot grouper

FIND

the answers to the quiz questions. Check your answers on pp. 92–93.

Quiz

1 What are the thin plates that cover most fish bodies called?

a. Fur
b. Skin
c. Scales
d. Muscles

2 Which body part helps the fish to breathe underwater?

a. Gills
b. Fins
c. Tails
d. Eyes

3 How long can the dwarf pygmy goby grow?

a. 11 in (29 cm)
b. 5 in (12 cm)
c. 2 in (5 cm)
d. ⅜ in (1 cm)

4 How many different species of fish are there in the world?

a. 1 million
b. Around 36,000
c. 25,000
d. Fewer than 5,000

super sharks

Some sharks are among the ocean's top predators. They are one of the most feared creatures on Earth. Amazingly, they've existed for more than 430 million years. That's longer than trees have been around!

a

b

c

1 Thresher shark
Thresher sharks are easy to recognize because their tail fins can be longer than their bodies. They rarely attack humans.

2 Sand tiger shark
The sand tiger shark is quite docile. The top part of its body is brownish gray with dark spots scattered around. Its belly is white in color.

3 Hammerhead shark
The strangely shaped head of the hammerhead shark helps it search the water for food. With an eye on either side of its head, it has a good range of sight.

Facts about...

Great white sharks

With the most powerful bite force of any shark, and a strong sense of smell, the **great white shark** is one of the most fearsome predators in any of the world's oceans.

MATCH

each shark to the description. Check your answers on pp. 92–93.

d

f

e

4 Goblin shark
The goblin shark lives in deep water and has protruding jaws. Its long nose has sensitive pit organs to detect prey in the dark.

5 Blue shark
The blue shark has a long, slender body and is an extremely fast swimmer. Its upper body is blue and the underside is white.

6 Whale shark
Despite being more than 59 ft (18 m) long, whale sharks are harmless to humans. Each whale shark has a different pattern of spots on its body.

Gallery of rays

Gliding through the water as if they're flying rather than swimming, rays are closely related to sharks, and can be found in many of the Earth's oceans.

Southern stingray

This stingray's tail spine is very sharp and contains a strong venom.

Painted ray

This ray's light-and-dark, wavy pattern helps it blend into the gravel on the seabed.

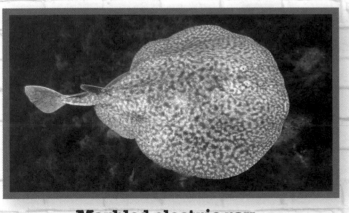

Marbled electric ray

This ray is capable of delivering an electric shock to defend itself.

Giant oceanic manta ray

The largest species of ray, it has a wingspan of up to 23 ft (7 m).

Spotted eagle ray

The spotted eagle ray swims through the water by moving its huge pectoral fins like the wings of a bird when flying.

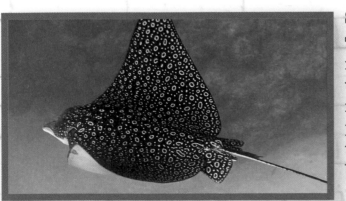

DRAW
the picture on the top-right onto the blank canvas below it.

Facts about...

Stings

Not all rays have venomous stings on their tails, such as the **manta ray and butterfly ray**. The manta ray is also known to have the biggest brain among ocean fish.

Found near coral reefs, the blue-spotted ribbontail ray has bright blue spots on its body.

Draw and Learn

35

They're not fish?

Just like whales, dolphins are actually marine mammals that live in the water but need to come up to the surface to breathe.

GUESS
if the statements are true or false. Check your answers on pp. 92–93.

Facts about...

Echolocation

By sending clicking sounds through the water, a dolphin can **"see with sound."** When sound waves created by the clicks hit an object, a signal bounces back to the dolphin.

Click

Click

Click

Did you know that dolphins are closely related to whales?

36

Bottlenose dolphins are the biggest dolphins in the world.

1
Dolphins only eat seaweed.

2
Dolphins have large brains, and are one of the most intelligent creatures on Earth.

3
With their streamlined bodies, dolphins can swim at speeds of up to 311 mph (500 kph).

4
A dolphin breathes through the blowhole on top of its head.

5
Dolphins travel around the oceans in groups called "pods."

6
Dolphins are so intelligent that some are able to understand human sign language.

Cute and cuddly?

Dolphins are sociable and playful animals who are friendly to humans, but they aren't harmless. They are very aggressive hunters of fish, squid, and even some sharks.

Predators

Grouping up helps to protect fish from predators such as the ones below, because only the fish on the outside of the group are exposed.

Bluefin tuna

These massive hunters can live for up to 40 years in the wild.

Shortfin mako shark

A relative of the great white shark, the mako can swim at speeds up to 46 mph (74 kph).

Indo-Pacific sailfish

The fastest fish in the ocean, the Indo-Pacific sailfish can swim at speeds up to 68 mph (110 kph).

Back to school

Smaller fish often swim together in large groups called schools or shoals as a way to protect themselves from bigger fish and other predators. It is also easier to search for food when part of such large groups.

A school of yellowstripe scad swimming close together.

COUNT

the number of fish in the image on the right. Check your answers on pp. 92-93.

Shoal

A shoal is a group of fish that swims in an uncoordinated way. It may contain different types of fish. A school of fish, however, is more organized, and contains the same type of fish.

seeing with sound

Some whales and dolphins use a technique called echolocation to find their way. To do this, they send out sound waves that are reflected back to them from objects in their path, creating a "map" that helps them to navigate.

READ

the clues and draw whales on the six squares where the rest of the pod is hiding.

This beluga whale's pod has split up and is scattered around the Arctic. It will need to use echolocation to find them again.

1 Find the school of **fish** near the bottom right. From there, go up two squares.

2 From the iceberg where the **polar bears** are playing, go up one square and then right three.

3 Look for the **ship**. From there, go right three squares and then down two.

Human technology called sonar is used on ships and submarines to locate objects—it works in the same way as echolocation.

Facts about...

Sea canaries

Belugas are called "sea canaries" because they are **very vocal**. They communicate with each other using various chirps, squeaks, and whistles.

3

4

5

6

4 One of the belugas can be found in the square one space to the right of the **submarine**.

5 Find the **narwhals** with their long tusks, go up two squares, and then right one.

6 Look for the **seals** lounging on the ice. From there go down one square and left two.

41

Fish defense

The underwater world is full of dangers, especially for fish that are killed and eaten by larger ones. To protect themselves from predators, some of these fish have unusual forms of defense.

FIND the answers to the quiz questions. Check your answers on pp. 92–93.

Lancet

Surgeonfish

The surgeonfish has two sharp, bladelike structures, called lancets, in front of the tail fin. When a predator is near, the surgeonfish uses the lancets in defense if attacked.

Facts about...

Luminous organs

Many creatures have luminous organs in the dark depths of the ocean. Clever predators, they can use their light to **lure in and attack their prey**.

Puffer fish

The puffer fish protects itself in many ways. It can inflate its body, which erects spines, so it looks bigger to a predator. The spines also make it difficult to swallow. Most puffer fish are poisonous.

Lionfish

The lionfish has 17 venomous spines in its fins. Those who get pricked by it can usually feel the pain for almost a week.

Quiz

1. Which fish inflates itself to look bigger to a predator?

2. What are the surgeonfish's bladelike structures called?

3. How many venomous spines does the lionfish have?

4. Which fish looks like a rock and has venom in its spines?

Stonefish

The blotched, bumpy body of the stonefish helps it blend in with the rocks and sand of the seabed. When it senses danger, the fish raises the venomous spines along its back for protection.

Wonderful whales

Whales may look like big fish, but they're actually mammals like us. They spend most of their time underwater, but they have to come up to the surface to breathe.

a

MATCH
the whales to their descriptions. Check your answers on pp.92–93.

 b

Whale oil

During the 19th century, people used to boil the **blubber** (fat) of whales to make oil. It had many uses, but was mostly used to light oil lamps.

1 Famous for its long tusk, the **narwhal** is found in cold Arctic waters. Males have tusks measuring up to 10 ft (3 m). Some females also have tusks, but these are shorter.

c

2 The **humpback whale** makes a series of repetitive clicks, whistles, and pulsed calls to make a melodic "whale song." Unlike other whales, it has long flippers that measure about 16 ft (5 m).

3 The **right whale** has portions of raised skin on its head, called callosites. There are three species of right whales: Southern Atlantic, North Atlantic, and North Pacific.

d

4 Not only is the **blue whale** the biggest species of whale, but it's also the biggest species of any animal! It can grow as long as 108 ft (33 m).

5 White in color and small for a whale, the **beluga whale** lives in cold Arctic and subarctic waters. This social animal usually travels in "pods" of up to 10 whales.

e

45

Monsters of the deep

The ocean can look calm on the surface, but many fearsome creatures lurk under the waves. Some of them not only look huge and menacing, but they are also quite dangerous!

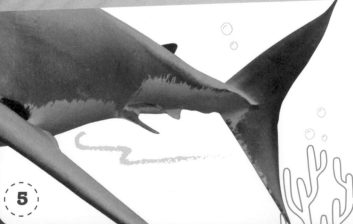

1

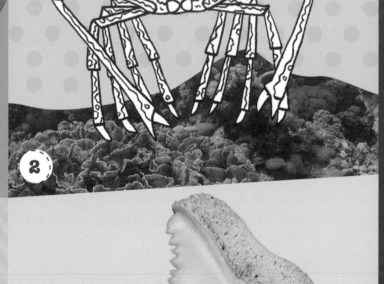

2

3

4

5

6

FIND
where these pictures are on pp. 48–67.
Check your answers on pp. 92–93.

7

8

9

10

11

12

Deep sea creatures

The bottom of the ocean is extremely cold and dark. Still, it is home to many mysterious fish and other animals—some of which can even glow in the pitch-black darkness.

Fangtooth

Cockatoo squid

Viperfish

Sea pig

COLOR in these sea creatures swimming in the depths of the ocean.

Facts about...

Unexplored ocean

More than 80 percent of Earth's oceans are still unexplored, most of which is the deep sea. This is because of the **darkness, freezing temperatures, and crushing levels of pressure**.

Gulper eel

Whalefish

Anglerfish

Cookie-cutter shark

Giant sea spider

Yeti crab

Ocean exploration

People can explore the underwater world through scuba diving, snorkeling, or deep-diving submersibles (underwater vehicles). These vehicles have windows through which marine life can be seen.

SPOT

seven differences between the two scenes shown above. Check your answers on pp. 92-93.

Shark senses

Like humans, sharks have five major senses—hearing, smell, sight, taste, and touch. However, they have an extra "electrical sense" that helps them hunt prey by detecting the electrical currents made by their heartbeats and muscle movements.

FIND the answers to the quiz questions. Check your answers on pp. 92–93.

Its snout has pores that can even detect prey hidden in the sand on the seabed.

Sharks have sharp eyesight.

Sharks can smell the scent of fish in the water that flows into their nostrils, and they follow this to hunt their prey.

The tastebuds are inside the mouth and not on the tongue.

The ears of a shark are not visible. Some sharks can hear sounds over a mile away.

Facts about...

The tapetum

Sharks can see well even when there isn't enough light. This is because of a layer of **special cells** called the tapetum. Cats also have a tapetum that makes their eyes look shiny in the dark.

Quiz

1 How many senses does a shark have?

a. 4
b. 6
c. 9
d. 12

2 Where are the shark's tastebuds located on its body?

a. Snout
b. Mouth
c. Fins
d. Tongue

Sharks can detect pressure changes and movement in water through a line of special cells in their skin called lateral lines.

3 Name the layer of cells that helps sharks see well in dim light.

a. Retina
b. Conjunctiva
c. Tapetum
d. Sclera

A toothy surprise

Teeth are one of the first things that come to mind when we think of sharks. Some sharks have long and razor-sharp teeth, making them one of the top predators of the ocean.

GUESS if these statements are true or false. Answers on pp. 92–93.

The sand tiger shark is also known as the ragged-tooth shark.

Facts about...

Rows of teeth

Most sharks have several rows of teeth so that when the front teeth wear down and fall out, they're replaced by ones **from the rows behind**. This happens throughout a shark's life.

1. The shortfin mako shark has needlelike teeth that point forward.

2. Every two days, the sand tiger shark is likely to replace a tooth.

3. The jaws of the great white shark are not firmly attached to its skull, so it can push its jaws out and take a big bite.

4. Sharks with teeth use them to rip and tear their prey, rather than to chew.

5. Megalodon, a prehistoric shark, had the biggest shark teeth. These were about 10 in (25 cm) long.

Types of teeth

Almost any shark tooth is bound to be sharp, but their shapes can be varied. Depending on the species and the food they eat, sharks' teeth can be long and pointed, triangular with bladelike edges, or flattened for crushing prey.

Record breakers

The world's oceans are full of amazing creatures in a variety of shapes and sizes. A few of them are truly remarkable and have fascinating traits. Let's read about some of them.

Fastest fish

The Indo-Pacific sailfish, known for the fin that runs along its back, is capable of swimming at speeds of more than 68 mph (110 kph) over short periods.

Deadliest shark

Growing to up to 20 ft (6 m) long and weighing up to 2,645 lb (1,200 kg), the great white shark has the most powerful bite force of any species of shark.

Biggest crustacean

Found in the Pacific Ocean near Japan, the Japanese spider crab can grow to up to 13 ft (4 m), from the tip of one front claw to the other.

Facts about...

Beluga caviar

Beluga caviar comes from the beluga sturgeon, found in the Caspian Sea. This caviar is one of the **most expensive foods** on Earth.

Beluga sturgeon

COLOR
the marine animals floating and swimming in the ocean.

Longest glider
The flying fish is able to use its fins to leap up to 33 ft (10 m) out of the water and glide for distances of up to 655 ft (200 m).

Biggest jellyfish
The lion's mane jellyfish can grow to up to 121 ft (37 m), from its top to the bottom of its tentacles. It is found in the cool waters of the Atlantic, Pacific, and Arctic oceans.

Longest life
In 2006, an ocean quahog (a clam) was discovered that was an estimated 507 years old, making it the oldest individual creature known to humans.

Loudest animal
Not only is the blue whale the largest animal on Earth, but it's also the loudest. It can make sounds as loud as a plane taking off!

Observing
orcas

Orcas, or killer whales, are large mammals that usually live in the colder areas of the ocean. Despite their name, these whales are actually the largest members of the dolphin family.

Orcas can weigh up to 14,550 lb (6,600 kg).

In black and white

Orcas are easily recognizable from their black-and-white markings. Every orca has a gray mark behind its dorsal fin that can be used to identify it. The fin itself can vary in shape and size, depending on the orca's age, gender, and location.

Facts about...

Orca diets
Orcas can grow up to 33 ft (10 m) long. They eat about 3–4 percent of their body weight each day. Their diet mainly consists of **seals, fish, and squid**.

Orcas talk to each other with clicks, whistles, calls, pops, and claps.

Orcas swim at speeds of up to 28 mph (45 kph) for short durations.

True or false?

GUESS
if these statements
are true or false.
Answers on
pp. 92–93.

1 The brain of an orca is 10 times bigger than a human brain.

2 Orcas that live in different parts of the ocean have regional accents to the sound of their clicks and whistles.

3 When swimming, orcas can keep one half of their brain awake, while the other half sleeps.

4 Orcas hunt polar bears as their prey.

The male orca has a bigger dorsal fin than the female.

Connect the dots to reveal the picture and then color it in.

Sea nettles

Sea nettles are species of jellyfish commonly found in both **Pacific and Atlantic oceans**. They feed on small marine creatures.

Blue jellyfish

Named for their **deep blue** color, blue jellyfish are often found washed up on beaches.

Facts about...

Strange beings

Jellyfish are some of the most unusual creatures on the planet. They're **made mostly of water**, and don't have brains, hearts, bones, or blood!

Things that sting

Jellyfish might look quite fragile—but they can be very dangerous! Their tentacles can deliver deadly stings that can paralyze and even kill.

Compass jellyfish

The compass jellyfish usually has a pattern of **32 brown lobes** around its edge and **16 V-shaped marks** on its bell.

Box jellyfish

The box jellyfish may look relaxed and beautiful, but some species contain **enough toxin to kill 60 humans.**

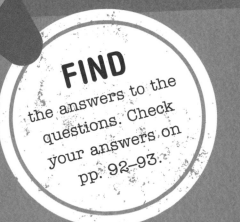

FIND the answers to the questions. Check your answers on pp. 92–93.

 1 What does the sea nettle feed on?

 2 How many humans could be killed by the toxin of some box jellyfish species?

 3 How does the blue jellyfish get its name?

4 How many brown lobes and V-shaped marks does a compass jellyfish have?

DRAW
the picture below onto the next page. Try starting in the corners.

Battle of the deep

Down in the murky depths of the twilight zone, two mighty giants battle it out for survival.

Sperm whale

After taking in air from the surface, the sperm whale dives into the darkness to hunt for giant squid, but it isn't always that easy. Sperm whales have been found with deep scars caused by the suckers on the squid's tentacles.

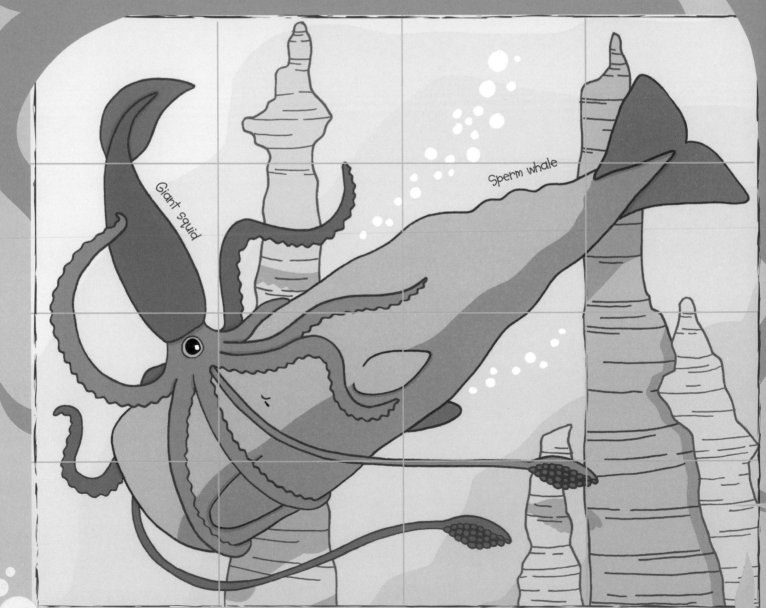

Giant squid

Sperm whale

The giant squid has the largest eyes of any animal on Earth.

Squid

Squid, also known as **cephalopods**, have eight arms and two tentacles. To swim, they suck water into their bodies and then shoot it out. This propels their bodies backward.

Giant squid

Most squid are around 2 ft (60 cm) long, but the giant squid can grow to up to 43 ft (13 m). It lives so deep in the ocean that it wasn't until 2005 that humans first saw one in their natural environment.

GUESS

if the statements are true or false. Answers on pp. 92–93.

1

Great whites can sense electrical signals in the water.

2

The lifespan of a great white shark in the wild can be up to 30 years.

Alpha predator

Movies and books make the great white shark seem scarier than it really is. But with its razor-sharp teeth and powerful, agile body, the great white shark is one of the ocean's most skillful hunters.

Facts about...

Biggest shark?

The great white is a large shark, but it's not the biggest one! The **whale shark** can grow to more than twice the size of the great white, but it's very docile and lacks sharp teeth.

The great white's massive jaws can contain about 300 teeth.

3

The great white shark can grow to a massive 20 ft (6 m) long.

4

More people are struck by lightning each year than are attacked by great white sharks.

5

Great whites can smell even the smallest drop of blood in water from several miles away.

Cruise control

A great white shark's body is shaped like a torpedo. This allows it to swim efficiently for a long time and switch to high bursts of speed when needed.

Great whites often attack their prey from below.

Feeling crabby

Known mostly for their shells and claws, crabs are crustaceans like lobsters and shrimp. Most crabs are amphibious, which means they can survive both on land and in the sea.

Fiddler crab

Male fiddler crabs are easy to spot because one of their claws is much bigger than the other.

Hermit crab

Without a hardened shell of their own, these crabs climb into the empty shells of other animals.

Shore crab

Shore crabs can be found on many types of seashore, including salt marshes and rocky shores.

Arrow crab

Arrow crabs are known for their arrow-shaped head and body, and long, thin legs.

DRAW the other half of the crab and then color it in.

Aquatic wonders

The ocean is so huge and brimming with life that it's hard to imagine all the amazing species that live there. How many do you recognize?

1

2

3

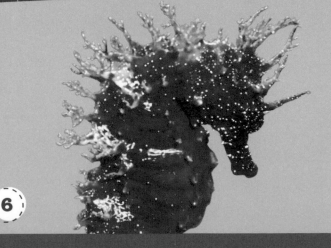

4

5

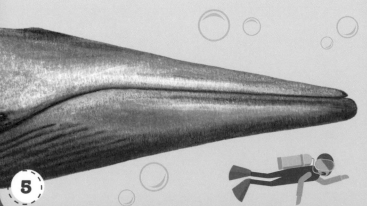

6

FIND
where these pictures are on pp. 70–91. Check your answers on pp. 92–93.

8

7

9

10

11

12

Sunlit zone

The top 656 ft (200 m) of the ocean is called the **sunlit zone** as it gets the most heat and sunlight. It's because of this that almost 90 percent of marine species, including the ones found below, live there.

MATCH the sea creatures to their descriptions. Check your answers on pp. 92–93.

I am one of the fastest swimming sharks in the world.

a

b

I swim upright in water.

The slimy mucus on my body protects me from stings.

c

Facts about...

Ocean pressure

Another reason most marine life lives close to the surface is that the **pressure rises as you get deeper**, making conditions difficult to survive.

(1) **Clown fish** are white and orange in color. They live among the stinging tentacles of sea anemones without being hurt.

(2) **Green turtles** feed on seagrass in warm, shallow lagoons. The largest green turtle ever found weighed 871 lb (395 kg).

(3) **Monk seals** are mammals. Hawaiian monk seals spend two-thirds of their time at sea hunting for food and playing.

(4) **Manatees** are large mammals that graze on algae, water grasses, and weeds.

(5) **Bull sharks** are fast and strong. They stalk the shallow waters eating fish, dolphins, and other sharks.

(6) **Seahorses** curl their tails around seaweed and corals to prevent themselves from being swept away.

d

Swimming around in shallow waters is so much fun!

f

I am a herbivore and live in shallow waters.

e

I am also known as a "sea cow."

71

Big blue

Growing to up to 105 ft (32 m) long, the blue whale is the world's largest animal. It's so big that it's hard to imagine without comparing it to other things.

FIND the answers to the quiz questions. Check your answers on pp. 92–93.

Human for scale

A very big appetite

Blue whales are so big that they need to eat up to 8,818 lb (4,000 kg) of krill (tiny shrimplike animals) every single day.

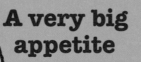

Facts about...

Gentle giant

You might think something so huge would be a fierce hunter, but blue whales **don't even have teeth**! They eat by filtering food through hard plates called baleen.

Not a big fish

Just like humans, dogs, and elephants, blue whales are mammals. It might seem unbelievable, but whales are more closely related to humans than they are to sharks, for example.

Quiz

1 How much krill do blue whales need to eat every day?

2 How much can the blue whale's heart weigh?

3 What are the hard plates that filter food for a blue whale called?

4 On average, a blue whale weighs as much as how many male Asian elephants?

The blue whale's heart can weigh up to 992 lb (450 kg). It has the largest heart in the animal kingdom.

An average blue whale can weigh more than 145 tons (131 metric tons)—as much as 26 male Asian elephants.

73

Tropical fish

Found in warm, shallow waters, tropical fish come in an incredible array of bright colors, and are one of nature's prettiest sights.

Fights between two of these fish can last for hours.

Pretty pets

Because tropical fish are so colorful, they are popular to keep as pets. However, their tanks need to be kept at **special conditions**, so they can be hard to look after.

Parrotfish nibble coral and poop out the grains as white sand. One parrotfish can produce 992 lb (450 kg) of sand in a year!

Color variety

Many scientists believe the reason tropical fish are so varied in color is that it helps them to identify a mate more easily among all the other species.

Moorish idol

Angelfish

Four-striped damselfish

Clown fish

Parrotfish

Seahorse

Puffer fish

Do not count the ones in the box.

COUNT

each type of fish you can see above. Check your answers on pp. 92–93.

I belong to a group of animals called "cephalopods."

Odd
octopuses

Like something from another planet, octopuses are one of the most unusual and interesting creatures in the world.

Strange biology

While they're most famous for their tentacles, octopuses are unlike any other sea creature in many ways.

An octopus has **three hearts**. Its **blood is blue** in color.

READ and learn all about this eight-armed marine creature.

TRUE OR FALSE?
OCTOPUSES LIVE FOR MORE THAN EIGHT YEARS.

The **suckers** on the tentacles of an octopus contain thousands of chemical receptors that help it to feel and taste.

An inky surprise

Most octopuses can release a **cloud of dark ink** from a special sac. This dark cloud hides the octopus while it makes its getaway.

There are 289 species of octopus living in the world's oceans.

The average lifespan of an octopus is around **1 to 5 years**.

Octopuses can change the color and texture of their skin to blend into their surroundings and hide from predators.

They **don't have any bones** so even large octopuses are able to squeeze through tiny gaps.

The octopus has strong suckers.

An octopus **moves backward** at high speeds in the ocean when scared. It draws water into its body, then squirts it out from a tube under its head. This propels the octopus backward in the water.

Big brains

Octopuses are believed to be **very intelligent**. They have good memories, and can even solve maze puzzles.

Help the seahorse

A male seahorse has been separated from his babies. Find something to use as a counter and help find his baby seahorses.

Start
Roll a dice and move the correct number of spaces along the board.

1

2 You flicker your back fin to swim in the water. **MOVE FORWARD** two spaces.

14 No danger lies ahead! Swiftly **MOVE FORWARD** two spaces.

15

16

13

17

18 A crab is moving toward you. You quickly change your skin color and blend in with the seagrass to avoid being hunted. **MISS A TURN.**

19

20

21 You stay close to the seagrass for protection. **GO BACK** to step 19.

3

4

5

6

It's mealtime!
You come across some
brine shrimp and suck
them up your snout.
MISS A TURN.

7

8

11

9

12

10

A strong
wave makes you
lose your balance.
Use your tail to hold
on to a seagrass stem.
ROLL AGAIN.

22

23

24

Hooray! You
spot your
children at last.
**ROLL A SIX TO
END THE GAME.**

A salmon's journey

The life cycle of an Atlantic salmon is remarkable. After years of living in the ocean, it embarks on a journey back to the very same river where it was born, thousands of miles away.

COLOR the rest of the pictures to finish the salmon's journey.

Facts about...

Getting home

Many scientists believe that one of the ways salmon are able to find their way back to where they spawned is by using the **Earth's magnetic field**.

1 It begins with female salmon **depositing eggs** in gravel nests on riverbeds for the males to fertilize. Some species of male salmon fish turn red, which may indicate they are ready for this to happen. Soon after the eggs are laid, most salmon die.

4 Heading back thousands of miles to the opening of the rivers where they were born, the salmon **battle upstream** against the strong currents, and even up and over waterfalls.

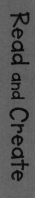

2 The babies hatch under the gravel and feed from a yolk sac until they are big enough to swim downriver **toward the ocean**. Along the way, young salmon undergo changes, including color and body shape, which will help them adapt to life in the ocean.

3 The salmon enter the sea and complete their development into adult fish. Here they travel together in schools, feeding on smaller fish, shrimp, and small squid. After a few years they begin their long **journey home**.

5 Along the way they have to avoid hungry fishermen, brown bears, and eagles. It's a very **long, hard trip**, and many of the salmon won't survive.

6 Exhausted, the salmon that manage to beat the odds and safely make it home will deposit and fertilize their eggs so that the cycle can **start again**.

Super powers

The ocean is home to lots of unusual creatures with strange abilities. In fact, many of these abilities are so strange, they seem no less than super powers!

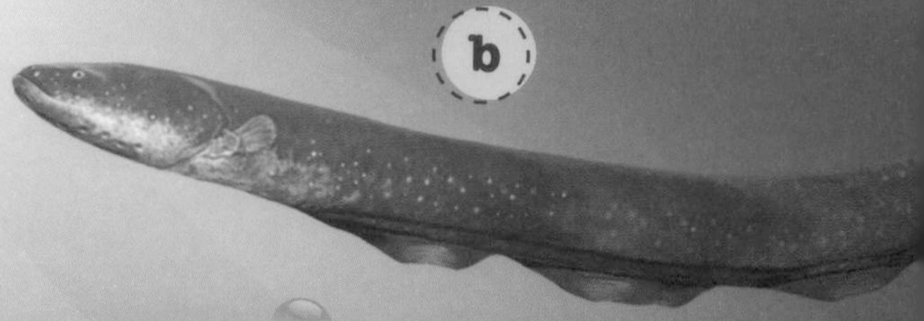

b

a

c

d

e

1 Mantis shrimp

The mantis shrimp might look harmless, but it packs a punch so fast and powerful it strikes like a bullet. There are more than 520 known species of mantis shrimp in the world. They come in shades of brown, bright green, and many other vivid colors.

Facts about...

Sea cucumbers

Sea cucumbers can survive in very deep water. They can **practically liquefy their bodies** as they push themselves into holes to hide from predators.

2 Flying fish

While flying fish can't actually fly, they can use their long finlike wings to glide above the surface of the water for up to 656 ft (200 m) at a time.

3 Electric eels

Electric eels have snakelike bodies, but they are neither snakes nor eels. They are, in fact, a type of knife fish. They can produce electrical discharges in their bodies that stun and kill their enemies.

4 Sea stars

Most sea stars are excellent healers. They can repair their damaged limbs and even sometimes regrow whole new ones. Sea stars usually have five limbs, but there are some that have a total of 50!

5 Cuttlefish

Cuttlefish have special cells that allow them to change color instantly. They do this to attract mates, confuse prey, and show how they are feeling. Cuttlefish have eight arms and two tentacles.

MATCH

the ocean creatures to their pictures. Check your answers on pp. 92–93.

Turtle dash!

While sea turtles live in the water, they're actually born on land. During nesting season, a huge amount of female turtles come ashore to lay and bury their eggs.

Raccoon   Fox

Seagull

START

1

2

3

4

Race to the ocean

Female turtles crawl out of the ocean to lay and bury their eggs in a sandy nest. A few months later, the eggs hatch and the babies scuttle down to the water as quickly as they can. There is danger all around since predators such as raccoons and foxes eat the eggs, while crabs and seagulls feed on the hatchlings.

FIND
which path takes the baby turtles to the ocean. Look out for dead ends!

Ghost crab

FINISH

Facts about...

Survival rate
Even if a baby turtle makes it to the sea, the **chances of survival** are low. Sharks, fish, and seabirds feed on baby turtles, so only a few survive to adulthood.

sea slugs

Unlike the slugs found on land, sea slugs are bright and colorful creatures. Sea slugs are picky eaters and they usually like to feed on sponges and soft corals.

Chromodoris annae
This colorful sea slug can be found in Indo-Pacific waters. It likes to feed on sponges. Chromodoris annae is also known as Anna's sea slug.

Spanish dancer
The Spanish dancer is one the largest sea slugs. When it swims in the ocean, its bright and flattened body looks a lot like a flamenco dancer from Spain. This is how it gets its name.

Spanish shawl
The striking Spanish shawl sea slug likes to eat hydroids, sea anemones, and gorgonian corals. The orange projections on its back act as a warning to predators that it doesn't taste very good.

Sea bunny
This sea slug looks a lot like a rabbit with two black "ears." It retains the toxins contained in sponges that it feeds on. This makes the slug an unpleasant meal for its predators!

Create your own sea slug

DRAW your own sea slug and give it a name.

Blue dragon
The blue dragon sea slug can be found at the surface of coastal waters in the Pacific, Indian, and Atlantic oceans. Its blue coloring helps it merge well with the ocean waves to avoid predators.

Facts about...

Rhinophores
Sea slugs have **hornlike structures** on their heads called rhinophores. These structures help slugs find food by smelling and sensing chemicals in the water.

What do you know about marine animals?

Oceans and seas are vast habitats where many different animals spend all or most of their lives. Let's see how much you know about these incredible creatures, and whether you can separate the true facts from the false ones!

GUESS if the statements are true or false. Check your answers on pp. 92–93.

1
Californian sea lions are slow swimmers. Their top speed is about 2 mph (3 kph).

2
A male **tiger cardinal fish** carries the female's eggs in its mouth until they hatch.

6
A **hermit crab** looks for empty sea snail shells to move into.

Facts about...

Land and sea

Californian sea lions spend their lives both on land and under the waves. When they dive in water, their nostrils automatically close. This allows them to **hold their breath for about 10 minutes**.

3

An average **reef manta ray** can eat 31 lb (14 kg) of plankton in a day.

4

Male **sea turtles** hatch from eggs that are laid in sands that are below 81.8 °F (27.7 °C).

5

A **sea star's** eyes are located at the ends of its arms.

Mythical creatures

Oceans and seas are not only home to marvelous creatures, they are also the breeding grounds of many myths and legends about magical beings and beasts.

MATCH the mythical creatures to their pictures. Check your answers on pp. 92–93.

a

b

Facts about...

Water deities

From **Neptune**, the Roman god of water, to **Kamohoalii**, the shape-shifting shark god from Hawaii, water deities have been worshipped in cultures all over the world.

c

d

① Zaratan
This **mythical sea turtle** is so huge that it is often mistaken for an island in legends and stories. The zaratan is said to sleep for 10 years at a time.

② Kraken
The massive kraken haunted the dreams of many sailors in the old days. A giant, **squid-like monster**, the mythical kraken has the ability to completely entangle a ship and break it in two.

③ Leviathan
This dreaded **sea serpent** is believed to devour ships and cause chaos. Hence, it is also called "Hellmouth."

④ Merpeople
There are several variations of merpeople in cultures around the world. In many of these tales, merpeople are described as being **half-fish** and **half-human**.

Answers

6–7

1. Page 12
2. Page 16
3. Page 8
4. Page 24
5. Page 14
6. Page 18
7. Page 20
8. Pages 18–19
9. Page 23
10. Page 16
11. Pages 16–17
12. Page 11

8–9

1. **False**. At least 50 percent of the world's oxygen is produced in the ocean.
2. **True**
3. **False**. The tusk is a tooth.
4. **True**
5. **True**
6. **False**. Pods can have up to 55 individuals.
7. **True**
8. **False**. It can weigh about 21 tons (19 metric tons).

10–11

1. Antarctica
2. Arctic Ocean
3. 36,070 ft (10,994 m)
4. 20 percent
5. Indian Ocean

12–13

True or False?
True

14–15

1. Arctic and Southern oceans
2. Open ocean
3. Underwater gardens
4. On rocky shores

20–21

1. a; 2. d;
3. a; 4. c

22–23

True or False?
False. The sunlit zone is the most well-lit zone.

26–27

1. Page 36
2. Page 33
3. Pages 42–43
4. Page 34
5. Page 33
6. Page 41
7. Page 40
8. Page 29
9. Page 35
10. Page 42
11. Page 31
12. Pages 38–39

28–29

1. c; 2. d; 3. g; 4. e;
5. a; 6. b; 7. f

30–31

1. c; 2. a;
3. d; 4. b

32–33

1. b; 2. e; 3. d;
4. c; 5. f; 6. a

36–37

1. **False**. Dolphins mostly eat fish, squid, and shrimp.
2. **True**
3. **False**. They can swim at speeds of up to 25 mph (40 kph).
4. **True**
5. **True**
6. **True**

38–39

19 fish

42–43

1. Puffer fish
2. Lancets
3. 17
4. Stonefish

44–45

1. c; 2. d; 3. a;
4. e; 5. b

46–47
1. Page 54
2. Pages 56–57
3. Page 49
4. Page 64
5. Page 53
6. Page 58
7. Page 65
8. Page 62
9. Pages 50–51
10. Page 55
11. Page 60
12. Page 63

50–51
1. Number of orca's flippers
2. Number of angelfish
3. Direction of jellyfish
4. Sea star
5. Color of seahorse
6. Top part of coral
7. Number of clown fish near the top of the coral

52–53
1. b; 2. b; 3. c

54–55
1. **False**. The teeth point backward.
2. **True**
3. **True**
4. **True**
5. **False**. The teeth were up to 7 in (18 cm) long.

58–59
1. **False**. It's about four times bigger.
2. **True**
3. **True**
4. **False**. Orcas hunt seals by pushing them into the sea.

60–61
1. Small marine creatures
2. 60
3. It's deep blue in color
4. 32 brown lobes around its edge and 16 V-shaped marks on its bell

64–65
1. **True**
2. **False**. It can be over 70 years.
3. **True**
4. **True**
5. **False**. They can smell blood from a mile or less at most.

68–69
1. Page 71
2. Page 74
3. Page 81
4. Page 82
5. Pages 72–73
6. Page 70
7. Page 82
8. Page 76
9. Page 71
10. Page 74
11. Page 73
12. Page 84

70–71
1. c; 2. d; 3. f;
4. e; 5. a; 6. b

72–73
1. 8,812 lb (4,000 kg)
2. It can weigh up to 992 lb (450 kg)
3. Baleen plates
4. 26

74–75
Moorish idol: 1
Seahorses: 2
Angelfish: 3
Parrotfish: 4
Four-striped damselfish: 5
Puffer fish: 6
Clown fish: 7

76–77
True or False?
False. They can live for up to 5 years.

82–83
1. d; 2. c; 3. b; 4. e; 5. a

88–89
1. **False**. They can reach speeds of 25–30 mph (40–48 kph)
2. **True**
3. **False**. It eats up to 66 lb (30 kg) of plankton in a single day.
4. **True**
5. **True**
6. **True**

90–91
1. c; 2. d; 3. b; 4. a

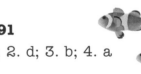

Glossary

agile
Ability to move quickly and easily

antifreeze
Natural substance produced by polar animals to protect their internal parts from freezing at low temperatures

array
Display or range of a certain thing

bell
The umbrellalike body of a jellyfish

blotched
Covered with irregular markings

caviar
Eggs of sturgeon fish that are preserved in salt and eaten as food

colony
Group of the same animals that live together

crustaceans
Animals that are mostly aquatic, have two pairs of antennae, and legs that branch into two. Crabs, lobsters, and shrimp are crustaceans

dorsal fin
A fin on the back of some aquatic animals

echolocation
Technique employed by some animals, such as dolphins, that uses reflected sound to locate objects, and determine how big and far away they are

entangle
To twist together or get caught in

fragile
Delicate or easily destroyed

glide
Movement without any propulsion

hatch
Process by which an animal breaks out of an egg

inflate
To make something bigger by filling it with air or water

lagoon
Area of shallow, saline water separated from the sea by a narrow barrier, such as a reef or sand bar

luminous
Shines or glows in the dark

magnetic field
invisible force field around a magnetic object, such as the Earth's interior, used by migrating animals (for instance sea turtles) to help them find their way

mammal
Warm-blooded animal that gives birth to live young, which are fed with milk produced by their mother

mate
An animal's partner

mythical
Something imaginary or
fictitious that exists
in ancient stories

paralyze
To make unable to move

predator
An animal that hunts
other animals for food

propel
To use a force to
cause movement

protruding
Sticking out from a
surrounding surface

radar
System that uses radio
waves to detect the location
of objects

receptor
Part of the body that
picks up information

serrated
Having a sharp,
jagged edge

spawn
Production of eggs and sperm
by aquatic animals

torpedo
A long, narrow weapon
fired under the water from
a submarine or a ship that
explodes when it hits a
target ship

translucent
Semitransparent. Allows
some light but no detail
to pass through

trench
A long, narrow depression
on the seafloor

tusk
Long tooth that extends
beyond the mouth of
walruses, narwhals,
and a few land animals

wingspan
Distance between the tips
of a pair of wings

Acknowledgments

Original edition: Design Clare Shedden, Sadie Thomas, Stefan Georgiou, Samantha Richiardi, and Kathryn Wilding; **Editorial** James Mitchem, Carrie Love, and Laura Palosuo; **US Editor** Margaret Parrish; **Illustration** Helen Dodsworth, Jake McDonald, and Dan Woodger; **Consultant** David Burnie.

DK would like to thank: Syed Tuba Javed and Kritika Gupta for editorial support; Mohd Zishan for design support; and Phil Hunt for proofreading.

The publisher would like to thank the following for their kind permission to reproduce their photographs:

(Key: a-above; b-below/bottom; c-center; f-far; l-left; r-right; t-top)

1 Dreamstime.com: Bennymarty (bl); Johannesk (tl). **4 Dreamstime. com:** Voislav Kolevski (br); Robyn Mackenzie / Robynmac (t). **Shutterstock.com:** cynoclub (tr). **6 Dorling Kindersley:** Linda Pitkin (crb). **Dreamstime.com:** Heather Rose (bl); Nico Smit / Ecophoto (cla). **7 Alamy Stock Photo:** Nature Picture Library / David Shale (clb). **Dreamstime.com:** Artur Kutskyi (tl/background); Christopher Wood (tl). **8 Dreamstime.com:** Planetfelicity (cl); Seadam (cra). **8-9 Dreamstime.com:** Piboon Srimak (cb). **9 Dreamstime.com:** Simone Gatterwe / Smgirly (tc). **10-11 Dorling Kindersley:** Linda Pitkin (ca). **11 Dreamstime.com:** Oleksandra Sosnovska (br). **12 Dorling Kindersley:** David Peart (c/jellyfish); Linda Pitkin (c, clb, cb, cb/worm, crb). **Dreamstime.com:** Dirk-jan Mattaar (fclb); Nico Smit / Ecophoto (cr). **12-13 Dorling Kindersley:** David Peart. **13 Alamy Stock Photo:** Genevieve Vallee (ca). **Dorling Kindersley:** Stephen Oliver (c); Frank Greenaway / Weymouth Sea Life Centre (cla); Linda Pitkin (c/Feather); David Peart (crb). **Dreamstime.com:** Mikhail Blajenov (ca/urchin); Tomstack7 (tr). **Getty Images:** Photographer's Choice RF / Peter Pinnock (cr). **14 Dreamstime.com:** Antoine Beyeler (b); Heather Rose (cl). **15 Alamy Stock Photo:** Nature Picture Library / Nick Upton (tr). **Getty Images / iStock:** goinyk (cl). **22 Alamy Stock Photo:** Juniors Bildarchiv GmbH / Buerkel, D.L. / juniors@wildlife (ca); Thomas Reavill (crb). **22-23 Fotolia:** rolffimages. **23 Alamy Stock Photo:** Lee Dalton (cl); Nature Picture Library / David Shale (bc). **Dreamstime.com:** Yiu Tung Lee (cra). **Getty Images / iStock:** LeoPatrizi (tl). **24 Alamy Stock Photo:** Travis VanDenBerg (cra). **Dorling Kindersley:** Linda Pitkin (cla). **Dreamstime.com:** Elisei Shafer (br). **26 Alamy Stock Photo:** Nature Picture Library / Alex Mustard (cra). **Dreamstime.com:** Vladvitek (clb). **Getty Images / iStock:** Artyustudio (cra). **27 Alamy Stock Photo:** Panoramic Images (cr); Richardom (cl). **Dreamstime.com:** Baramee Temboonkiat (br). **Science Photo Library:** Patrick Landmann (cr). **28 Alamy Stock Photo:** Steve Morgan (crb). **Getty Images / iStock:** E+ / EXTREME-PHOTOGRAPHER (cla); E+ / piola666 (bc). **28-29 Getty Images / iStock:** Zocha_K (Background). **29 Alamy Stock Photo:** Kip Evans (crb). **Dreamstime.com:** Jonmilnes (cra). **Getty Images / iStock:** E+ / SolStock (bl). **Science Photo Library:** Patrick Landmann (tr). **30 Dreamstime.com:** Bennymarty (c). **31 Dreamstime.com:** Wrangel (cl). **Fotolia:** uwimages (cla). **33 Getty Images / iStock:** Artyustudio (tr). **34 Alamy Stock Photo:** Helmut Corneli (cr); Nature Picture Library / Alex Mustard (cra); Nature Picture Library / Sue Daly (cra, cl). **Dreamstime.com:** Sonyaillustration (fbl). **Getty Images / iStock:** Tomasz Dutkiewicz (bl). **34-35 Dreamstime.com:** Lichaoshu. **35 Alamy Stock Photo:** Richardom (cr). **Dreamstime.com:** Marilyn Barbone (bl); Sonyaillustration (fbr); R. Gino Santa Maria / Shutterfree, Llc (br). **38-39 Dreamstime.com:** Baramee Temboonkiat. **39 Dreamstime.com:** Seadam (crb). **40-41 Fotolia:** rolffimages. **42 Alamy Stock Photo:** imageBROKER.com GmbH & Co. KG / Norbert Probst (cl); Panoramic Images (crb). **43 Dreamstime.com:** Vladvitek (t); Wrangel (b). **44-45 Fotolia:** rolffimages. **46 Alamy Stock Photo:** Nature Picture Library / Sue Daly (tr). **Dreamstime.com:** Paul Vinten (cla). **Shutterstock.com:** BW Folsom (crb). **47 Alamy Stock Photo:** Nature Picture Library / Linda Pitkin / 2020VISION (bl). **Dorling Kindersley:** Colin Keates / Natural History Museum, London (crb). **48-49 Dreamstime.com:** Andreykuzmin. **50-51 Alamy Stock Photo:** Artur Golbert (x13). **Dreamstime.com:** Andreykuzmin (window). **50 123RF.com:** anterovium (cr); Pavlo Vakhrushev / vapi (ca). **Shutterstock.com:** cynoclub (cla). **51 123RF.com:** anterovium (cr); Pavlo Vakhrushev / vapi (ca). **Alamy Stock Photo:** Nature Picture Library / Sue Daly (cb). **Dreamstime.com:** Tetiana Kozachok (cla/diver). **Shutterstock.com:** cynoclub (ca/x2). **52 Dreamstime.com:** Picsfive (tl). **52-53 Alamy Stock Photo:** mauritius images GmbH / Reinhard Dirscherl. **Dreamstime.com:** Vicente Barcelo Varona (Background). **53 Dreamstime.com:** Ian Andreiev (x3); Picsfive (tr). **54 Dreamstime.com:** Paul Vinten (bl). **55 Dorling Kindersley:** Colin Keates / Natural History Museum, London (clb, crb). **56-57 Fotolia:** rolffimages. **56 Dreamstime.com:** Irina Vershinskaya (bc). **60 123RF. com:** Pavlo Vakhrushev / vapi (ca/x2). **Alamy Stock Photo:** Nature Picture Library / Linda Pitkin / 2020VISION (tr). **61 Alamy Stock Photo:** Sabena Jane Blackbird (cra). **Getty Images / iStock:** Jake Davies (tl); t_kimura (br). **64-65 Fotolia:** rolffimages. **64 Shutterstock. com:** BW Folsom (bc). **66 Dorling Kindersley:** Linda Pitkin (crb). **Dreamstime.com:** Linusy (fbl); Harald Schmidt (clb); Shamils (bl). **Shutterstock.com:** Seth Yarkony (cra). **67 Dreamstime.com:** Linusy

(fbr); Anton Starikov. **68 Alamy Stock Photo:** amana images inc. / UMI NO KAZE / a.collectionRF (cl); WILDLIFE GmbH (bl). **Dorling Kindersley:** Harry Taylor / Natural History Museum, London (cla); Linda Pitkin (cra). **Dreamstime.com:** Voislav Kolevski (br); Photographerlondon (crb). **Fotolia:** Strezhnev Pavel (tl). **69 Alamy Stock Photo:** David Fleetham (clb); Artur Golbert (cr/x4); Melba Photo Agency (cla); Martin Strmiska (cb). **70-71 Alamy Stock Photo:** amana images inc. / UMI NO KAZE / a.collectionRF (b). **Fotolia:** Strezhnev Pavel. **70 Dreamstime.com:** Voislav Kolevski (clb). **Getty Images / iStock:** MediaProduction (c). **71 Alamy Stock Photo:** David Fleetham (crb). **Dorling Kindersley:** Harry Taylor / Natural History Museum, London (b). **Dreamstime.com:** Hotshotsworldwide (c). **72-73 Alamy Stock Photo:** WILDLIFE GmbH. **74-75 Alamy Stock Photo:** Artur Golbert (clownfishx2); Martin Strmiska (coralX2). **Dorling Kindersley:** Linda Pitkin (Parrotfishx5). **Dreamstime.com:** Johannesk (Moorish Idol X2); Voislav Kolevski (Damselfishx6). **Fotolia:** Strezhnev Pavel (Background). **Shutterstock.com:** cynoclub (Angelfishx4). **75 123RF.com:** anterovium (sea-horsex3). **76-77 Getty Images:** Stuart Westmorland. **78 Dreamstime.com:** Evgenii Naumov (ca). **78-79 Dorling Kindersley:** David Peart. **79 Dreamstime.com:** Evgenii Naumov (br/X4). **80-81 Fotolia:** rolffimages. **82 Alamy Stock Photo:** Melba Photo Agency (bc); SeaTops (crb). **Dreamstime. com:** Photographerlondon (cla). **Shutterstock.com:** Dotted Yeti (tr). **82-83 Alamy Stock Photo:** amana images inc. / UMI NO KAZE / a. collectionRF (Backckground). **Fotolia:** Strezhnev Pavel (Background). **85 Dreamstime.com:** Igor Zakowski (tl). **86 Alamy Stock Photo:** imageBROKER.com GmbH & Co. KG / Norbert Probst (cl); Poelzer Wolfgang (cra); Photo Network / Joanne Huemoeller (clb). **Dreamstime.com:** Tartilastock. **Shutterstock.com:** Phiseksit (crb). **88 Alamy Stock Photo:** Robertharding / Michael Nolan (cl). **Dreamstime.com:** Isselee (bc); Paul Vinten (cra); Valerijs Novickis (b/Background). **88-89 Alamy Stock Photo:** amana images inc. / UMI NO KAZE / a.collectionRF (Seaweed). **Getty Images / iStock:** Katatonia82 (Ocean surface). **Shutterstock.com:** Rich Carey. **89 Alamy Stock Photo:** Biosphoto / Sergio Hanquet (crb). **Dreamstime.com:** Richard Carey (cr); Lotophagi (bc). **Getty Images / iStock:** MediaProduction (t). **90 Dreamstime.com:** Liudmyla Klymenko (c). **Shutterstock.com:** Kostiukart (c). **90-91 Getty Images / iStock:** LiuNian (Background). **92 Dreamstime.com:** TravelFaery (br). **Getty Images / iStock:** Artyustudio (tr). **93 Dreamstime.com:** Evgenii Naumov (br/X4). **95 Alamy Stock Photo:** Melba Photo Agency (br). **Getty Images / iStock:** Vladone (tc)

Cover images: *Front:* **123RF.com:** anterovium clb; **Alamy Stock Photo:** Melba Photo Agency c; **Dorling Kindersley:** Jerry Young cra; **Dreamstime.com:** Bennymarty bc, Tomstack7 crb; **Fotolia:** uwimages cb; *Back:* **Dorling Kindersley:** Jerry Young tl, bc; **Dreamstime.com:** Yiu Tung Lee crb; *Spine:* **123RF.com:** anterovium cb; **Dreamstime.com:** Wrangel t

All other images © Dorling Kindersley